Greater Than a Tourist – Nizhny Novgorod Russia

50 Travel Tips from a Local

> TOURIST

Linh Le

Lock Haven, PA

ISBN: **ISBN:** 9781521365748

DEDICATION

This book is dedicated to my love and our great time together in Nizhny.

BOOK DESCRIPTION

Are you excited about planning your next trip?
Do you want to try something new while traveling?
Would you like some guidance from a local?

If you answered yes to any of these questions, then this book is just for you.

Greater Than a Tourist – Nizhny Novgorod Russia by Linh Le offers the inside scope on Nizhny Novgorod.
Most travel books tell you how to travel like a tourist. Although there's nothing wrong with that, as a part of the Greater than a Tourist series this book will give you tips and a bunch of ideas from someone who lives at your next travel destination.

In these pages you'll discover local advice that will help you throughout your stay. Greater than a tourist is a series of travel books written by locals. Travel like a local. Get the inside scope. Slow down, stay in one place, take your time, get to know the people and the culture of a place. Try some things off the beaten path with guidance. Patronize local business and vendors when you travel. Be willing to try something new and have the travel experience of a lifetime.

By the time you finish this book, you will be excited to travel to your next destination.

So grab YOUR copy today. You'll be glad you did.

Ten cents of each book purchased is donated to teaching and learning.

CONTENTS

15. Have a Look at the Major Street in Nizhny - Bolshaya Pokrovskaya Street

16. Take a Stroll Along the Second Major Street in Nizhny - Rozhdestvenskaya Street

17. Witness the Most Beautiful Church in Nizhny with Your Own Eyes

18. Become an Artist on Pokrovka

19. Feel the Fresh Air in an Industrialized City

20. Walk to "Switzerland"?

21. Do the Rides

22. Go to Limpopo, One of the Biggest Private Zoos in Europe

23. Take Some Good Photos of Churches and Cathedrals

24. Experience European Movies

25. Find out About the Kremlin!

26. Ride a Cable Car in Nizhny

27. Have the Best Deal for Visiting Museums

28. Feel the Russian Spirit – Have Fun at Nizhny Novgorod Fair

29. "Meet at Chkalov"

30. Climb Chkalov Staircase

31. Visit Rukavishnikov's Mansion

32. Touch the Lucky Sculptures in Nizhny

33. Get Away to the Village of Big Boldino with its Famous Golden Autumn

Author Bio

Linh Le is a representative of Vietnamese culture, who moved to Russia at the age of six. She is grateful to life for an opportunity to have spent more than seventeen years surrounded by Slavic culture up to this moment. Being a Linguistics University graduate, Linh has always been keen on learning about customs and traditions of different countries. She adores travelling and has been to five countries, nineteen cities so far...

Linh enjoys exploring the world around her and sharing all this knowledge with those, who might need it. She is a foodie and a cat lover.

.

WELCOME TO > TOURIST

WHY AM I A LOCAL?

Being raised in Russia, I have always considered it my home. Having lived in Nizhny for four most beautiful years in my life, in the place where I studied, worked and found love, I can most definitely assume that I am a local.

Nizhny Novgorod is an extraordinary city in Russia and one can never find anything like this anywhere! Nizhny is quite a big city with highly developed economy and technology, but at the same time it tries to prolong its unique old-fashioned spirit, which can never fade in course of time. The city contains totally different elements and blends them together, turning itself into an original and exquisite city of federal importance.

Nizhny can offer everyone something that would suit them. With its large number of entertaining places, parks, cafes and restaurants, the city will never let anyone be bored within its territories.

I love Nizhny for its eagerness to take an irreplaceable part in the heart of everyone who has ever visited it. Believe it or not, but once you visit this city, you will never be the same again.

1. Choose the Best Way to Get to Nizhny

Nizhny Novgorod, also known as "pocket of Russia" is an easy place to get to. There's an international airport in the city that you could use for your trip. You can also get here by taking high-speed trains known as "Lastochka" (swallow) and "Strizh" (swift). Travelling by train in Russia might be quite an adventure, however these two kinds of trains are very comfortable and they start their routes from the capital. This is also a good opportunity for you to stop in Moscow for a couple of days or more and get to know its sightseeings, often represented as symbols of the country. The trains run during the day, so you can enjoy the picturesque sights of Russia on your way to Nizhny as well.

2. Pick Your Clothes According to the Local Weather

Nizhny Novgorod is a very beautiful city, situated on the intersection of two great Russian rivers – the Volga and the Oka. Therefore the city is separated into two parts: uptown (located on the hills) and downtown (from the other side of the hills). These two parts are connected with several bridges. Downtown is always colder than uptown due to the wind from the rivers. And you should choose your clothes for Nizhny depending on the season and having in mind the this difference between uptown and downtown. Nizhny Novgorod has four seasons of a year in all their beauty. There is much snow in winter and the temperature is about - 20 0 C (-4 0 F), but it is really hot in summer too. The average temperature in summer is approximately +25 0 C (77 0 F).

3. Find a Nice Place to Stay

If you are lucky to have any friends, who live in Nizhny Novgorod, you should definitely let them know of your arrival. Perhaps, they could invite you for a stay or ask around for their friends to take you in. However, if you don't have any acquaintances from the city, don't feel bad as in our modern world there are so many available ways of finding places to stay in another country. The simplest one is obviously couchsurfing, which is totally free of charge. With couchsurfing you can live with a local and experience the Russian way of life. Although, if you don't like staying with strangers then, perhaps, that's not your cup of tea. There's a web-site booking.com, that offers a wide range of hostels, motels, hotels and etc. On this web-site you can find the cheapest and the most expensive places in the city. Always read the comments and reviews, besides, pay attention to the ratings as well.

4. Get to the Centre of the City the Easiest Way

The first place that you should visit is definitely the center of the city. Most of the sightseeings are located exactly there, once you get to the center, they will be within walking distance. If you decide to go to the centre right away after the flight, then you can use

-bus №11 to the metro station "Park Kultury" (Park of Culture), then got to the metro and get to "Gorkovskaya" station;

-bus №20 to "Moskovsky vokzal" (Moscow railroad station), then got to the metro and get to "Gorkovskaya" station;

-minibus №46 that will take you straight to Minin and Pozharsky square.

If you're getting to the center from the downtown, better use the metro. Everything costs 20 rubles per one ride per person.

5. *Mind your Manners While Taking a Public Transport*

The peculiar characteristic about Nizhny Novgorod in the sphere of transport communication comparing to other cities of Russia is that you have to wave your hand to get on a minibus. Do it as if you are hitchhiking, but unlike tourists, residents of the city do this on a regular basis. Russians pay much attention to the manners, especially in public transport. If you are a man, don't forget to let ladies and children enter the vehicle first. Being inside the vehicle, offer your seat to older people, women or children. If you see an older person, you should offer your seat regardless of your gender.

6. Learn Basic Words and Phrases in Russian

People in Russia usually learn English at school, but to be honest, there is still room for improvement. You will need Russian if you want to buy something, ask the route or need any kind of help that involves engaging a conversation. The Russian language might seem difficult at first sight, but for basic exchange of information I think you only need 2-3 months of learning it for interactions with the locals. There are many free videos online that would assist you in this process. Duolingo has interactive lessons of Russian as well, but using one method alone won't be enough, at least combine two different sources. Make sure to learn at least greetings, numbers, question words and pronouns before going to Russia.

7. Never Shorten the Name to "Novgorod", Only "Nizhny"!

Residents of Nizhny Novgorod are very proud of their history. Although there is another city, similar to Nizhny Novgorod by name, it is Veliky Novgorod (which means Novgorod the Great). Sometimes people from other cities in Russia shorten "Nizhny Novgorod" to "Novgorod", but that is a mistake, as it is the shortened version of "Veliky Novgorod". People get confused once you make this mistake and some of them can even be offended by such an innocent error. Residents of Nizhny Novgorod have their own term "nizhegorodets" for a resident male and "nizhegorodka" for a resident female.

8. Get to Know the City's History

The territory of Nizhny Novgorod was once inhabited with Finno-Ugric tribes in the 9th century. The city itself was founded in 1221 by Georgy II Vsevolodovich. In 1611 the residents of the city under command of Minin and Pozharsky gathered militia to free Moscow from occupation. It was renamed to Gorky during Soviet Union times after a famous writer Maxim Gorky. The city became an industrialized center during Soviet times. During World War II the city produced a large amount of weapons and military equipment.

9. Have a Look at Nizhny Within the Frames of International Trade

The city has many opportunities for developing one's business. There is an international trade center in Nizhny Novgorod, which is one of the World Trade Centers Association. An international business summit is conducted at Nizhny Novgorod Fair annually. Such big companies as Intel, Samsung, Yandex, Gaz group and many others.

10. Be a Part of One of the Biggest Music Festivals in Russia

If you are a music fan, then you will find Nizhny Novgorod very chanting and attractive. There are many bands that give live shows weekly and many world-known artists visit this city (for example 30 Seconds to Mars, Scorpions, Placebo and etc.) every year. Besides, every summer, there is a spectacular electronic music festival, held in a village of Nizhny Novgorod Region, called Alfa Future People Festival (AFP). AFP is represented as a festival of technology and innovation. That is totally true, because everything inside the territory of the festival is very thematic. For instance, you can't pay for anything there with cash or usual credit cards. Every person gets a credit card and a watch synchronised to it and you can pay with your watch. According to statistics, in 2016 the festival included 5 scenes, 100 DJ's, 75 hectares of land and 50 000 viewers.

"I am not the same, having seen the moon shine on the other side of the world." — *Mary Anne Radmacher*

11. Become a Soccer Fan in Nizhny

Are you a soccer fan? If not, you might want to become one, as the upcoming World Cup (2018) will be held in Russia. Nizhny Novgorod will be honored to host several matches during this international event. For this purpose a new stadium is being built right now and it should be ready for 2017 FIFA Confederations Cup already. The stadium will be able greet 44 899 football fan on its territory, it will host two playoff matches, one ⅛ final match and one ¼ match final. Don't miss an event of the world level!

12. Explore the Beauty of Russian Ballet

Oh my god! Only these three words will come to your mind, once you get to see Russian ballet. It goes without saying, that ballet is one of the most well-known Russian symbols around the world. I think everybody has heard of Tchaikovsky and his "Swan Lake". Well, in Nizhny Novgorod you will definitely have a chance to witness such a legendary thing with your own eyes! Visit The Nizhny Novgorod State Academic Opera and Ballet Theatre. Besides ballet you can also get tickets to musicals, plays and opera. The place is well known for great performances, pleasant sounds and satisfying services. Once you go to the theatre don't forget to put on your fine clothes. It is not a must, but manners means a lot in Russia, once again.

13. Walk Along the Banks of Great Russian Rivers

The most beautiful place in Nizhny Novgorod, in my opinion, is a place where two great rivers intersect. This place also has the letter "Nizhny Novgorod" as Hollywood does. The letters are placed not on the hills though, but on a special platform under the hills. If you get up on the hills you will see the most picturesque view in Nizhny: the intersection of two rivers, a long bridge above them and Rozhdestvenskaya street with a pretty orthodox church ornamented in a traditional way. Take a stroll along the banks of these rivers and feel the atmosphere of Nizhny Novgorod!

14. Have Fun with Local Cruises

As Nizhny Novgorod is situated on two rivers, it is optimal for such kind of cities to have water activities. There are many kind of cruises in Nizhny, they could be both long-term and short-term. I'll concentrate more on short-term water trips, as they are easy affordable by price and by time. There is a company called "Водоходъ" that provides trips during the whole day. The duration is 1,5 hours and the price is 250 rubles per a ride for an adult and 150 rubles for a child. There are no onboard excursions during the trip, though, so you might want to study some information in advance. Some Russians can celebrate their birthday with such a trip so don't be surprised if somebody brings alcohol and drinks it onboard.

15. Have a Look at the Major Street in Nizhny - Bolshaya Pokrovskaya Street

Bolshaya Pokrovskaya Street, also known as "Pokrovka" is a major street in the city. It connects squares: Minin and Pozharsky Square, Theatre Square, Gorky Square and Lyadov Square. Bolshaya Pokrovskaya was considered to be noble till 1917 and was transformed into the major street at the end of 18th century. Pokrovka was fully reconstructed in 2004. bronze statues were set along both sides of the street. It is the busiest street in the city, especially at the weekends. You can meet many street musicians, poets, political, street artists, painters and many others. You can also buy souvenirs here, they don't cost much, even though it's the major street.

16. Take a Stroll Along the Second Major Street in Nizhny - Rozhdestvenskaya Street

Another street that you should definitely pay a visit to is Rozhdestvenskaya, that resembles "Pokrovka" in many ways. The street connects Square of National Unity with Annunciation Monastery. The most most famous sightseeing is Rozhdestvenskaya Church. There are many cafes and restaurants located here, but in my opinion these places are more expensive than those at Pokrovka. If you take a walk along Rozhdestvenskaya, you will feel the spirit of nobility due to old buildings situated here.

17. Witness the Most Beautiful Church in Nizhny with Your Own Eyes

The Church is one of the most beautiful architectural views in Nizhny Novgorod. The building has five cupolas that are built according to cardinal directions. The cupolas used to be green at first like Saint Basil's Cathedral in Moscow, but later on they were changed into golden. Unlike Saint Basil's Cathedral that is situated inside the Kremlin, the Rozhdestvenskaya Church is located on the street that bears the same name as the church. You can pay a visit to this splendid construction, while having a walk along Rozhdestvenskaya Street.

18. Become an Artist on Pokrovka

As it was mentioned before, Pokrovka as an artistic place, where everybody who wants to express themselves or reveal their talents can do that. People just come there with their musical instruments (a flute, a guitar, a violin, even a big harp!) to play as a street artist. One can often see professional musicians performing popular compositions or movie soundtracks. There are no restrictions on anybody, even if you don't know how to play an instrument or how to sing or how to dance with fire, you can simply recite a poem or think of a funny sheet of paper asking for money, put your hat in front of you and in some time people will start giving money. However, if you're an artist - that's definitely what I would strongly recommend you to do - play on Pokrovka to get to know how much Russian audience values your talents!

19. Feel the Fresh Air in an Industrialized City

Nizhny was known as an industrial city in the times of Soviet Union. It was a closed city that produced military machines and cars. After Soviet Union collapsed Nizhny didn't lose its function and many technological companies chose their offices in Russia to be located in Nizhny Novgorod (Intel, for instance). The population of the city is approximately 1 300 000, the traffic in the city is very busy in the mornings and afternoons. To tell the truth, good ecology is not a thing that Nizhny Novgorod is famous for, that's why local people pay attention to clean air. There are many parks in the city, you should definitely visit some of them such as: First of May Park of Leisure and Culture, Sormovo Park, Switzerland Recreation Park, Park of Victory and etc.

20. Walk to "Switzerland"

Such phrases as "Let's meet at "Switzerland" or "I'll see you in two hours at "Switzerland" are used pretty often in Nizhny. That sounds a little bit funny out of context, as "Switzerland" is a big local park that has many things there. It has various games, delicious treats and typical flora for a Russian park that reminds a forest very much. If you want to go for a picnic, this park is the place that you're looking for. "Switzerland" is so big, that it has a zoo inside. You can also visit the zoo and get acquainted with animals living in Russia, such as bears.

"The use of traveling is to regulate imagination with reality, and instead of thinking of how things may be, see them as they are." – Samuel Johnson

21. Do the Rides

The first place that you should visit for amusement rides should be "Switzerland" once again. The attractions are divided into two categories: for children and adults. If you will be travelling with children, there won't be any difficulty to find entertaining things to do for them in Nizhny. The games for adults are pretty much exciting. There is a ride called "octopus", a big wheel, a merry-go-round and many others. Besides, "Switzerland" there is another amusement park in Sormovo region that can provide you with more extreme kinds of rides. There is a zoo in that amusement park as well, so there's an alternative to "Switzerland" if you will live not that close to the center.

22. Go to Limpopo, One of the Biggest Private Zoos in Europe

The zoo was founded in 2003 and has 203 kinds of animals, that is 1300 creatures for exhibition. Limpopo is situated in Sormovo park and occupies 7,1 square hectares of land. Local people often organize different kinds of events and celebrations on the territory of the zoo. Limpopo used to have a contact zoo program, that allows children and adults to touch several kinds of animals. There are also many campaigns here, for instance, "Plant your own tree", that is conducted annually on October, 4 (World Animal Day). If you visit Limpopo, you'll have a chance to name a newborn animal if you win a game or competition there.

23. Take Some Good Photos of Churches and Cathedrals

Two things that every city in Russia must have are churches and cathedrals, as Russia is a very religious country. There are at least four buildings of this thematic that you should pay a visit to. They are Saint Alexander Nevsky Cathedral, Voznesensky Cathedral, Church of Nativity of Most Holy Mother of God and Saint Sergiy Radonezhsky Church. All these grand constructions represent Russian culture and its deep faith in Orthodox Church. The concept of Russian churches is also to look majestic both inside and outside the building, so if you have a chance to enter any of those churches, please do. Don't forget to cover your head with a scarf or something while entering a holy building.

24. Experience European Movies

Avant-garde cinematography is appreciated in Russia. There is a place in Nizhny Novgorod that shows rather non-commercial movies, in other words, not blockbusters, but high-intellectual keen European movies for everybody. "Orlyonok" ("an eaglet" in English) is the place where you can go to feel the current look of Europeans on the cinema. The cinema theatre shows different cinema festivals or competitions that are not broadcasted worldwide. One more advantage of this place is really cheap prices (twice cheaper than at a regular cinema theatre).

25. Find out About the Kremlin

If you think that there is only one Kremlin in Russia, you will find this info very surprising! In Russia you can at least count 20 of them! There is one in Nizhny Novgorod as well. The construction could be not that massive as the one in Moscow, but it is still worth paying attention to. The color of the Kremlin in Nizhny is red, as in the capital, and if you go there, you will discover an exhibition of war cars and planes there too.

26. Ride a Cable Car in Nizhny

Riding a cable car is very exciting! It is not very expensive (only 80 ruble per person per a ride) and you can see Nizhny from another angle. The cableway connects Nizhny and its neighbor town - Bor. While riding a cable car you can observe a unique picture over the Volga and see how Nizhny and its sightseeings come together in one picture.

27. Have the Best Deal for Visiting Museums

If you are not a local, you probably haven't heard of such a thing as Museum's Night in Nizhny Novgorod. The night is held once a year for everybody who want to visit the museums free of charge and didn't have an opportunity to do that before. Most of the museums will be open all night. This year (2017) museum night was on May, 20th and many museums participated in the event. Among them you can find such popular museums and sightseeings in Nizhny as Arsenal, the Kremlin, Regional Universal Scientific Library of Nizhny Novgorod, Museum Exhibition Complex, Nizhny Novgorod State Art Museum, Kladovka Art Gallery, Rukavishnikov's Mansion, Sandy Hobby Club, the State Russian Museum of photography, Sakharov Museum, Kashirin House (Maxim Gorky Childhood Museum) and many others. Don't miss this night if you have a chance!

28. Feel the Russian Spirit – Have Fun at Nizhny Novgorod Fair

Fairs and carnivals in Russia have always been an inseparable element of Russian culture from ancient times. Every city in Russia tries to secure its traditional spirit in every possible way. Nizhny Novgorod has a big fair that holds a great deal of events in its territory. It is situated in downtown and has always been specialized in both: retail and wholesale kinds of trade. Merchants from all parts of Russia and abroad came to this place to sell their goods. The Fair was so popular that it obtained its own culture, like having a built-in theatre, a circus and a show booth. Nowadays the Fair is an exhibition complex. Many international conferences and exhibitions are held here as the Fair looks very presentable and authentic.

29. "Meet at Chkalov"

Valery Pavlovich Chkalov was a legendary Russian aircraft test pilot, who accomplished the first nonstop flight from Moscow to Vancouver via the North Pole. Chkalov Monument was constructed by his friend, Isaac Abromovich Mendelevich on December 15, 1940, two years after Valery Pavlovich's death. Mendelevich got Stalin's Award for this job. On the surface of the pedestal one can see contours of the map of the Northern Hemisphere indicating the routes of flights of the heroic crew Chkalov - Baidukov - Belyakov to the Far East, and also to America via the North Pole. "Let's meet at Chkalov" is a very popular phrase in Nizhny Novgorod. It could either refer to Chkalov Monument or Chkalov Staircase.

30. Climb Chkalov Staircase

The view on Chkalov Staircase is one of the most spectacular ones in Nizhny Novgorod. The staircase consists of 560 steps and was one of the longest staircases in Russia. It connects the Upper Volga River Embankment with the Lower one. There are two viewing platforms in the places where staircases intersect. This is one of the most well-known sightseeings in Russia and it should definitely be a must in your list once you decide to visit Nizhny. There are many kinds of competitions held here, races, for instance. As the staircases is located next to the Kremlin, people come here with their children to enjoy the view, with their friends to have a picnic and with their love to have a nice date. If you get down to the lower embankment, it will be very easy for you to continue your journey with a river trip, as there are many places where they sell tickets for cruises over there.

*"Nobody can discover the world for somebody else.
Only when we discover it for ourselves does it
become common ground and a common bond and
we cease to be alone." – Wendell Berry*

31. Visit Rukavishnikov's Mansion

Rukavishnikov's mansion should be a vital item in your list of sightseeings worth visiting in Nizhny Novgorod. The building is considered to be one of the most beautiful and interesting construction of the 19th century. At first, the mansion belonged to a merchant Vezlomtsev, then Rukavishnikov obtained it in 1840-s. His heir, also a Rukavishnikov turned the mansion into a majestic palace in Italian style. In 1877 Rukavishnikov was considered to be the richest man in Nizhny Novgorod, so it's absolutely worth visiting a house of a former aristocrat in the city.

32. Touch the Lucky Sculptures in Nizhny

"Funny Goat" is a monument located on Pokrovka, the main street of the city. It is situated on the Theatre Square, where an annual festival is celebrated. The emblem of the event is a goat, so its location is not coincidental. The legend says that if you sit on the monument, grasp its horns and make a wish, then it will come true. However, judging by another layer of paint on the goat's udder one can say that people believe rubbing it much more effective than riding the goat. There's one more sculpture on Pokrovka worth seeing, it is a monument of Evgeniy Evstigneev, an actor of Soviet Union. People rub his nose, hoping for a prosperous life with much money.

33. Get Away to the Village of Big Boldino with its Famous Golden Autumn

Russian literature is well-known throughout all over the world. I'm sure you have heard of such surnames as Tolstoy, Pushkin and Dostoyevsky. Big Boldino is a place where Pushkin himself created his most acknowledged masterpieces such as "Eugene Onegin", "The Bronze Horseman", "The Queen of Spades" and many others. If you are Pushkin's fan, you'll discover many interesting thing here. There's a museum dedicated to Pushkin in the village, and I think that you shouldn't miss a chance of visiting it, because who knows, when this chance will ever come again!

34. Acknowledge How Happy You Are with Arch Electrical Vitamins!

"Electrical vitamins" is a trade mark that a local firm Redox uses to issue their products. The goods are promoted as something that can help someone to slow down their process of aging, improve their health and etc. According to the official web-site of the company electrical vitamins are "currents of skin-galvanic origin, created by closing of a low-resistance conductor irritable and not irritable conductor regions". That all sounds very vague for me, but what is interesting for tourists is the fact that the company has built an arch that claims to have an ability to measure your level of happiness. What you have to do is to step on under the roof and touch the both columns with your hands. You will see special iron plates on the columns. The arch has something resembling a clock on the top, and you'll have to ask somebody to tell you the digit, so that you could know how happy you are!

35. Examine Maxim Gorky's Places

As you know, Nizhny Novgorod was once called "Gorky", after the name of a Russian famous writer - Maxim Gorky. He was one of the most outstanding writers in Russia, Maxim Gorky was nominated of the Nobel Prize 5 times. His life was not an easy one. Maxim's real full name was actually Aleksey Maksimovich Peshkov. He was born in Nizhny Novgorod, became an orphan at the age of 11. After the death of his parents, Maxim was brought up by his grandmother, but he ran away at the age of 12 in 1880. Gorky tried to commit suicide in 1887, so as one can see by his biography, he didn't have a chance to enjoy a careless life. "Gorky" means "bitter" in Russian, an implication to the taste of life that he had tasted. There are many places in Nizhny Novgorod, dedicated to this outstanding author. First of all, there is Gorky Square at the very center of the city. Then there's a house, where he was born (address: Kovalikhinskaya, 33), a house where he spent his childhood (address: Pochtovy S'yezd, 21), a house where he moved to being at school (address: Korolenko, 42), a place where he worked being an 11-year-old (address: Maxim Gorky, 74), a place where he wrote (address: Semashko, 19) and many others.

36. What Food Should You Try in Nizhny?

Nizhny Novgorod is very popular among tourists for its cuisine, because it is a large city that can offer you a big variety of food. The best idea for you would be taking a stroll along two major streets in the city: Pokrovka and Rozhdestvenkaya street. Most of the famous cafes and restaurants with delicious food are located there. However, as these streets are most popular in Nizhny the prices are higher comparing to the rest of the city. Of course, the first thing to be mentioned is the Russian cuisine. Besides that, you should definitely try Caucasian (from the Caucasus region) kind of food, such as khachapuri, dolma and etc. Nizhny Novgorod has many places that offer sushi, wok and pizza. My recommendation would be to try sushi at Tanuki (big restaurant at the heart of the city, that has a good service), wok at Sovok (quite a cheap place, very popular among students) and pizza at Dodo (Russian net of pizza with transparent policy in everything, pizza is made of products of high quality).

37. To Eat or Not to Eat Burgers - That Is the Question

Besides sushi, wok and pizza, burgers are getting extreme popularity in the city recently. To tell the truth, burger in Nizhny are the best ones that I have ever tried in my life. Unlike the US, this is not a typical kind of food, so you might want to try the Russian way of cooking them. The first place that I would recommend for visiting is Salut. The best thing about these burgers is the juicy meat that melts in your mouth. My second recommendation would be Krasty Burgers. They have the longest list of burgers in the city and ingredients are not very typical for burgers. For instance, the place has a pilaf burger with buns made of rice! And my third recommendation would be Mitch. It is the most expensive burger place and what's special about it is the sauce, I guess. Mitch has such an exotic, in my opinion, ingredient in one of their burgers - a fried eel.

38. Check Out THE shawarma at Srednoy market

Of course, shawarma is not traditional Russian food, however there is one place in Nizhny that makes it so good, that people from all over the country come here to try it. It is located at Srednoy market, its price is only 70 rubles for a small one. The place is also well know for great sanitary norms, so you won't have to worry about the quality of the food. There's always a big line in front of the place and it is the first kiosk with the letters "Та самая шаурма", which literally means "The shawarma". What's so special about that shawarma are the sauce and the meat. The sauce is quite piquant, neither sweet, nor sour. The meat is smoky even if you order a shawarma with chicken, it is smoky as well. This is a definitely a must try thing in Nizhny!

39. Taste Some Kvass

This drink is a definitely a must try element if you go to Russia. People's opinion on kvass is rather contradictory. Some think that it's too weird, others can't resist drinking it all the time once having it tried. This is a traditional sour Slavic drink that is cooked on basis of fermented flour and grist or rye-bread. Moreover, kvass could also be used as broth in several kinds of soups, for example "okroshka", cold kvass soup with vegetables and cooked meat. It sure would taste really odd, but you only live once!

40. Visit One More Monument - Minin and Pozharsky

Minin and Pozharsky are historical personages. They were leaders of the Second People's Militia in the Time of Troubles. In Nizhny Novgorod one can find a monument dedicated to these two heroes. The monument is located at the end of Pokrovskaya street, opposite the Kremlin. There is also such a monument in the Kremlin in Moscow, as these two people were significant in Russian history. Moscow was occupied by Polish at the time. Minin started summoning people for rebellion and Pozharsky lead the process. The pose of the monument is very inspiring as most monuments in Russia.

"Happiness always looks small while you hold it in your hands, but let it go, and you learn at once how big and precious it is."

— Maxim Gorky

41. Get International with "Solyanka"

There are many foreigners in Nizhny Novgorod. Most of them are students, who came here to pursue their degree in Nizhny. There are also people, who came here for work and, undoubtedly, there are many tourists here as well. "Solyanka" is a non-commercial project created by "Sphera", a center for volunteers in Nizhny Novgorod. The aim of the project is to gather people who are interested in other languages / cultures / people in one place for them to get acquainted and talk to each other. Once you get there, you'll see a registration desk, where you're given stickers with languages that you can speak. This way people speaking the same language (s) could easily find each other. The project is not functioning during summer, so if you aren't visiting Nizhny Novgorod in summer, you should definitely drop by!

42. Observe the City of Many Religions

Russians are very religious people. Almost every person in Russia believes in God. It's a very personal question for everybody, but despite the strict restriction of Christianity (one God) people in Russia are open to all kinds of religions. There's an Indian temple in Nizhny, along with a mosque, synagogue and, of course, traditional Russian churches. In fact, the city is so open to new forms of religions, that Nizhny even has a church of the Flying Spaghetti Monster!

43. Find Out About Avtozavod - the Birthplace of Natalia Vodyanova

Have you ever heard of Natalia Vodyanova? She is a Russian supermodel philanthropist and actress, who was born in Nizhny Novgorod. In 2012 she was the third in Forbes' list of top-earning models in the world. There are different stories about her modest origin, stories of her selling products at local markets. Natalia is an inspiration for all the girls in Nizhny Novgorod. The region of her birth is called Avtozavod, known as a poor district in Nizhny Novgorod. It is located in downtown, formerly famous for a car factory. Unlike uptown Avtozavod doesn't have such popular sightseeings as the Kremlin, but it has a plenty of parks.

44. Sunbathe at a Local Beach

Not that many people spend their time on the beach in Nizhny Novgorod. There is a sandy island called Grebnev Sands, that is situated quite close to the center of the city. However, it would be problematic to sunbathe there, as the island is now a heritage, but you can visit it within a tour or excursion. If you want to sunbathe, you should go to a beach at Grebnoy Kanal. It is quite nice over there, a very good place to go to with your friends and family on a day-off. Its location is very convenient as well, as you won't have drive out of the city to reach the beach.

45. Do Some Shopping

Shopping is very an essential element of travelling, most women would say. Actually, some people travel to other places (for instance Milan or Paris) solely for this purpose. Well, being a big city Nizhny Novgorod possesses all these advantages in forms of big malls and shops on its territory as metropolises do. You can shop here and save some money, especially in the time of economic crisis in Russia. The currency dropped about twice its previous value, so you might be able to afford some things haute couture that you could allow yourself to indulge before. Firstly, you can go to a trading center "Fantastica". Almost all Nizhny goes there to buy either products or clothes. If you want to purchase brand things, go to Lobachevsky Plaza. Besides these two there are other ones, like Nebo, Chocolate, Zhar-ptitza and many others.

46. Enter the Magic World

Have you ever wanted to feel tiny as Alice in the Wonderland? Do you enjoy optical illusions? If you have answered either of these questions with a "yes", then you should definitely explore the magic buildings that Nizhny can offer. First of all it's the Museum of Illusions, where 3D pictures come to live. Don't forget to take your camera and make some photos there. Besides the Museum of Illusion you can also have fun at Giant's House, where everything is of a large size. Then you can go to mirror labyrinth, where it's quite hard to find a way out. Then there's ribbon labyrinth, but it's much easier than the mirror one, to my mind. If you like horror movies, then you should visit the Labyrinth of Fear. It's really scary in there!

47. Skate Anytime of the Year

Winter sports are very popular in Russian Federation. Such sports as hockey, skating and skiing are favored by Russian from a very young age. There are many skating rinks in Nizhny Novgorod and they work year round, so that you can enjoy skating even on a hot summer day. The most popular place in the town is Sports Palace, where hockey tournaments are held. There is a big skating-rink inside the building, so if you're a winter sports fan, then you should go there for sure!

48. Party with Nizhny

Nizhny Novgorod is a big city that has a great deal of entertaining places. Unlike Europe Russian clubs and bars work all night (usually till 6 p.m.). The most popular night club among the youth is Milo Concert Hall, that has many events during a week. There are different kinds of parties aimed at reaching various ages, subcultures and preferences in this club. Most of Russian celebrities have their shows and concerts at this rather small night club. If you are a fan of rock music, I think you should visit Rock Bar. They have a live music band to play for them every Friday They function as a usual cafe, that serves food and drinks during the day and their menu is adjusted for the night time as well. You can also visit Jam Prestige, The Top Club, Premio Centre and many other night theatres in Nizhny Novgorod.

49. Don't leave Nizhny without trying Russian cuisine!

Some traditional Russian dishes seem very odd to foreigners. You can actually try Russian cuisine almost everywhere. Just have a walk along either Bolshaya Pokrovskaya street or Rozhdestvenskaya street. The traditional dishes that I would recommend you to try are: borsch, dressed herring, blini (Russian crepes) with caviar, salo with brown bread, pierogi and pelmeni. Some of them are not traditional Russian, but either Belorussian or Ukranian, but these dishes are so popular in Russia, that some people think that it's all Russian. Borsch is Russian soup with beetroot, dressed herring is a salad with mayo, beetroot and salted herring, pierogi are Russian pies with different kinds of fillings and pelmeni are Russian meat dumplings. Never leave without trying the whole list of all this food!

50. What Should You Bring Home from Nizhny?

The city has always been known for its masters, who could create handcraft very delicately and meticulously. Souvenir shops usually have the craft of such masters. Their craft is usually made from wood and decorated manually to every last detail in their characteristic style. The things that are decorated by masters differ: it could be a matryoshka, could be a spoon, a fork, a dish, a chair and various other things that you can buy for your everyday life. Young ladies can purchase traditional lacy shawls that can further be used in your wardrobe. If you are a sweet tooth, you should defitely bring some traditional rooster-like lollipops, local marble and zephyr (something like marshmallow). And of course, a magnet for you fridge to remind you of such a pleasant place as Nizhny Novgorod!

> TOURIST

Greater than a Tourist

Please read other Greater than a Tourist Books.

Join the >Tourist Mailing List :
http://eepurl.com/cxspyf

Facebook:
https://www.facebook.com/GreaterThanATourist

Pinterest:
http://pinterest.com/GreaterThanATourist

Instagram:
http://Instagram.com/GreaterThanATourist

Please leave your honest review of this book on Amazon and Goodreads. Thank you.

77477375R00052

Made in the
USA
Columbia, SC